tes

ecclesiastes

or, the preacher

authorized king james version

grove press
new york

with an introduction by | doris lessing

The Pocket Canons were originally published in the U.K. in 1998 by Canongate Books, Ltd.
Published simultaneously in Canada
Printed in the United States of America

FIRST AMERICAN EDITION

Copyright information is on file with the Library of Congress
ISBN 0-8021-3614-1

Design by Paddy Cramsie

Grove Press
841 Broadway
New York, NY 10003

99 00 01 02   10 9 8 7 6 5 4 3 2 1

a note about pocket canons

The Authorized King James Version of the Bible, translated between 1603 and 1611, coincided with an extraordinary flowering of English literature. This version, more than any other, and possibly more than any other work in history, has had an influence in shaping the language we speak and write today. Presenting individual books from the Bible as separate volumes, as they were originally conceived, encourages the reader to approach them as literary works in their own right.

The first twelve books in this series encompass categories as diverse as history, fiction, philosophy, love poetry, and law. Each Pocket Canon also has its own introduction, specially commissioned from an impressive range of writers, which provides a personal interpretation of the text and explores its contemporary relevance.

Doris Lessing was born of British parents in Persia in 1919 and was taken to Southern Rhodesia when she was five. She arrived in England in 1949 with her first novel, The Grass is Singing, *which was published in 1950. Since then her international reputation, not only as a novelist but also as a non-fiction and short story writer, has flourished. She has won countless prizes and awards and some of her most celebrated novels include* The Golden Notebook, The Summer Before Dark, Memoirs of a Survivor *and the* Martha Quest *series. Her most recent works include* African Laughter *and two volumes of her autobiography,* Under My Skin *and* Walking in the Shade.

introduction by doris lessing

It is something of an undertaking, to write even a few words about a text that has inspired mountains of exegetics, commentaries, analyses, over so many centuries, and in so many languages: and you have not read one word. Immodesty, it could be called, and when I allow myself to think about my audacity, I do feel a little breeze of elation which, considered, turns out to be a mild attack of panic. But most readers will be in the same innocent condition, if they have read *Ecclesiastes* at all. Once, and not so long ago, everybody in Britain and for that matter everyone in the Christian world, was subjected to that obligation, going to church, where every Sunday was heard the thundering magnificence of this prose, and so, ever after, they would have been able to identify the origin of phrases and sayings which are as much a part of our language as Shakespeare. These days, if someone hears, 'There is a time to be born and a time to die ...' they probably do think it is Shakespeare, since the Bible these days is the experience of so few. Ecclesiastes? Who's he! But an innocent, even an ignorant, reader may discover a good deal by using simple observation.

The book begins with a description, 'The words of the

Preacher, the son of David, king in Jerusalem.' That is to say, the words have been collected from notes, or memories, of the Preacher, by disciples or pupils or friends, and made into a whole: probably after he was dead. He did not himself make this book, and it is tempting to remember that he said, 'Of the making of books there is no end, and much study is a weariness of the flesh.' Other great teachers, such as Socrates, Jesus, Confucius, many others, refrained from making books and testaments, leaving this task to other people. Why did they not see the necessity to preserve their 'image' or to edit a testament to make sure that posterity would see them as they saw themselves? Was the reason that they knew their influence – what they said, how they lived – had impressed their pupils and their contemporaries so strongly in their lifetimes that written records were superfluous? I think it is worthwhile to at least consider this possibility.

It is not until the twelfth verse that we hear his own words, with 'I, the Preacher, was king over Israel, in Jerusalem.' He tells us he devoted himself to the acquisition of wisdom, which is the task given to the sons of men by God, but there was pain in it. 'For in much wisdom there is much grief; and he that increaseth knowledge increaseth sorrow.' So then he decided to experience pleasure and the satisfactions of worldly accomplishment. He built houses and planted gardens and vineyards and orchards; he made pools and streams; he acquired male and female servants and all kinds of possessions, and silver and gold, and male and female singers. Whatever he had a fancy to have – so he tells us – he got; he was like the people now who decide that they are going to have a good time and not care about serious things. But then, having done all that, he had a good long look at his life and his property and his riches and knew it was all vanity and vexation of spirit (vanity in the sense of futility, illusion) and that happiness is not to be found in pleasure and that wisdom is better – making a full circle, one might say, if it were not that even a casual reading reveals that verse by verse this is contradictory stuff, a confusing message – if he ever intended what he said to be considered as a message. What we have here is sayings from different occasions, and different contexts, and with different people. There is a deep and terrible need in us all to systematise and make order, and perhaps it is helpful to imagine this material in a pre-book stage, when it was scribbled notes made when listening to the Preacher; or what happened when pupils met after he was dead: 'What do you remember of him? And you? And you?'

What unites the book, is precisely that this is some of the most wonderful English prose ever written. My father, young at a time when not to accept church religion was to invite persecution and social ostracism, said that Sundays, when he had to go to church three times, and also to Sunday school, was like a great black hole every week, but later said that it was listening to the prose of the Bible and the prayer book that taught him to love language and good literature. Generations of writers have been influenced by the rhythms of the Bible, which may be observed in the prose of the best of them – as well as the worst – and we are very much the poorer because the Bible is no longer a book to be found in every home, and heard every week.

We should remember that this prose was written to be heard as much as to be read. The difference between now and then is emphasised by the fact that people used to say, not, 'Let us go and see a play', but 'Let us hear a play'. Shakespeare was not long dead. Surely the translators of this Bible had that sea of sound in their ears, or had been influenced by it. Ears expected to be royally fed.

It was Latin that had been heard in churches. That means that for centuries the common people who did not know Latin did not understand what was going on up there between the priests and God. It is safe to assume they weren't listening much. And now, suddenly, with the translations into English, there was this feast of sound.

From the very first verse of *Ecclesiastes* you are carried along on a running tide of sound, incantatory, almost hypnotic, and it is easy to imagine yourself sitting among this man's pupils, listening to – for instance, 'Remember now thy creator in the days of thy youth, while the evil days come not, nor the years draw nigh when thou shalt say, I have no pleasure in them.' Your ears are entranced, but at the same time you are very much alert. You have to be old to understand that verse, to see your whole life, from early heedlessness to present regret for heedlessness; you find yourself drifting off into speculation. Was this particular admonition addressed to young people, to remind them that old age will come for them too? Or reserved for grey heads who would hear it with the ears of experience? Or flung out in an assembly, to be caught by anyone who could – who had the ears to hear, as Jesus put it.

Towards the end, verse 9 of chapter 12, suddenly it is not his voice, not 'I' speaking, and we are back to description; '… because the preacher was wise, he still taught the people knowledge; yea, he gave good heed, and sought out, and set in order many proverbs.' That is how one contributor to the book saw what Ecclesiastes was doing. And, yet again, we are reading a document that to us is ancient, but it records people who saw themselves as successors in a long line, stretching back into their antiquity.

Between the man, Ecclesiastes, and ourselves, are many veils. One is translation. Over the exact meaning of a word or phrase scholars have laboured and many sermons have been delivered in churches. That word 'Preacher' for instance. In what other ways could the original have been translated? 'Preacher' is so much a concept from organised Christianity, which spawned preachers by the thousand men (and now women) standing in pulpits to expound their views of life to a congregation, and their quite amazing intimacy with God's thinking. Should that 'Preacher' have been 'Teacher'? – a very different thing.

Spiritual teachers were and are part of the Eastern traditions, and that they are not part of ours is precisely because the concept of 'Preacher' was imposed instead – not the aspiration towards the experiential Path to God (or Jehovah, or Allah, or Buddha) but a passive congregation being lectured by God's Spokesman. Or Spokeswoman. *Do what you are told* – by priests, by mullahs.

Another barrier is the nature of the people who recorded the words, or who remembered them. We all know that what we say to a friend will be filtered through the character and experience of that person, and it is safe to assume that Ecclesiastes' pupils were not on the same level as he was, any more that Jesus's disciples were on his level, and that they, like us, had to strain to understand a nobility of mind that was beyond their ordinary selves. There is a little cry of despair in this text, the tale of a small city, besieged by a great king; a poor wise man saved the city, and yet no one remembered the poor man. 'Wisdom is better than strength' is the conclusion, 'nevertheless, the poor man's wisdom is despised and his words not heard.'

There is an interesting deduction or two to be made. This man was the son of David, that is to say, of the Royal House of David, at a time when kings were considered to be God-chosen and God-inspired. The word 'ecclesiastic' now means a clergyman, or describes a clergyman, or what appertains to churches. There is a little encapsulated history here: this 'Preacher' was no churchman, and nowhere does he mention a church: thus do the living springs of knowledge, of wisdom, become captured by institutions, and by churches of various kinds.

ecclesiastes or, the preacher

The words of the Preacher, the son of David, king in Jerusalem.

> ² 'Vanity of vanities,' saith the Preacher,
>> 'Vanity of vanities; all is vanity.
> ³ What profit hath a man of all his labour
>> which he taketh under the sun?
> ⁴ One generation passeth away,
>> and another generation cometh,
>>> but the earth abideth for ever.
> ⁵ The sun also ariseth, and the sun goeth down,
>> and hasteth to his place where he arose.
> ⁶ The wind goeth toward the south,
>> and turneth about unto the north;
>>> it whirleth about continually,
>> and the wind returneth again
>> according to his circuits.
> ⁷ All the rivers run into the sea; yet the sea is not full;
>> unto the place from whence the rivers come,
>>> thither they return again.
> ⁸ All things are full of labour; man cannot utter it.
>> The eye is not satisfied with seeing,
>>> nor the ear filled with hearing.
> ⁹ The thing that hath been, it is that which shall be;
>> and that which is done is that which shall be done;

and there is no new thing under the sun.

¹⁰ Is there any thing whereof it may be said,
"See, this is new"?
It hath been already of old time,
which was before us.

¹¹ There is no remembrance of former things;
neither shall there be any remembrance
of things that are to come
with those that shall come after.

¹² I the Preacher was king over Israel in Jerusalem.

¹³ And I gave my heart to seek and search out
by wisdom concerning all things
that are done under heaven;
this sore travail hath God given
to the sons of man to be exercised therewith.

¹⁴ I have seen all the works that are done under the sun;
and, behold, all is vanity and vexation of spirit.

¹⁵ That which is crooked cannot be made straight,
and that which is wanting cannot be numbered.

¹⁶ I communed with mine own heart, saying,
"Lo, I am come to great estate,
and have gotten more wisdom than all they
that have been before me in Jerusalem;
yea, my heart had great experience
of wisdom and knowledge."

¹⁷ And I gave my heart to know wisdom,
and to know madness and folly.
I perceived that this also is vexation of spirit.

¹⁸ For in much wisdom is much grief;
and he that increaseth knowledge increaseth sorrow.

2 'I said in mine heart,
    "Go to now, I will prove thee with mirth,
        therefore enjoy pleasure,"
    and, behold, this also is vanity.
² I said of laughter, "It is mad"
    and of mirth, "What doeth it?"
³ I sought in mine heart to give myself unto wine,
    yet acquainting mine heart with wisdom;
        and to lay hold on folly,
    till I might see what was that good
        for the sons of men,
    which they should do under the heaven
        all the days of their life.
⁴ I made me great works; I builded me houses;
    I planted me vineyards:
⁵ I made me gardens and orchards,
    and I planted trees in them of all kind of fruits.
⁶ I made me pools of water, to water therewith
    the wood that bringeth forth trees.
⁷ I got me servants and maidens,
    and had servants born in my house;
        also I had great possessions
    of great and small cattle
        above all that were in Jerusalem before me.
⁸ I gathered me also silver and gold, and
    the peculiar treasure of kings and of the provinces.
        I gat me men singers and women singers,
    and the delights of the sons of men,
        as musical instruments, and that of all sorts.
⁹ So I was great, and increased more

than all that were before me in Jerusalem;
　　　also my wisdom remained with me.
¹⁰And whatsoever mine eyes desired
　　I kept not from them,
　　　　I withheld not my heart from any joy,
　　for my heart rejoiced in all my labour,
　　　　and this was my portion of all my labour.
¹¹Then I looked on all the works
　　that my hands had wrought,
　　　　and on the labour that I had laboured to do,
　　and, behold, all was vanity and vexation of spirit,
　　　　and there was no profit under the sun.
¹²And I turned myself to behold wisdom,
　　and madness, and folly:
　　　　for what can the man do
　　that cometh after the king?
　　　　Even that which hath been already done.
¹³Then I saw that wisdom excelleth folly,
　　as far as light excelleth darkness.
¹⁴The wise man's eyes are in his head;
　　but the fool walketh in darkness:
　　　　and I myself perceived also
　　that one event happeneth to them all.
¹⁵Then said I in my heart,
　　"As it happeneth to the fool,
　　　　so it happeneth even to me;
　　and why was I then more wise?"
　　　　Then I said in my heart, that this also is vanity.
¹⁶For there is no remembrance of the wise
　　more than of the fool for ever;

seeing that which now is in the days to come
shall all be forgotten.

And how dieth the wise man?

As the fool.

17 Therefore I hated life;
because the work that is wrought under the sun
is grievous unto me,
for all is vanity and vexation of spirit.

18 Yea, I hated all my labour
which I had taken under the sun,
because I should leave it unto the man
that shall be after me.

19 And who knoweth whether he shall be
a wise man or a fool?

Yet shall he have rule over all my labour
wherein I have laboured,
and wherein I have shewed myself
wise under the sun. This is also vanity.

20 Therefore I went about to cause my heart to despair
of all the labour which I took under the sun.

21 For there is a man whose labour is in wisdom,
and in knowledge, and in equity;
yet to a man that hath not laboured therein
shall he leave it for his portion.

This also is vanity and a great evil.

22 For what hath man of all his labour,
and of the vexation of his heart,
wherein he hath laboured under the sun?

23 For all his days are sorrows, and his travail grief;
yea, his heart taketh not rest in the night.

This is also vanity.
²⁴ There is nothing better for a man,
    than that he should eat and drink,
        and that he should make his soul
enjoy good in his labour.
    This also I saw,
    that it was from the hand of God.
²⁵ For who can eat,
    or who else can hasten hereunto, more than I?
²⁶ For God giveth to a man that is good in his sight
    wisdom, and knowledge, and joy,
        but to the sinner he giveth travail,
    to gather and to heap up,
        that he may give to him
    that is good before God.
        This also is vanity and vexation of spirit.

3

'To every thing there is a season,
    and a time to every purpose under the heaven:
² a time to be born, and a time to die;
    a time to plant, and a time to pluck up
        that which is planted;
³ a time to kill, and a time to heal;
    a time to break down, and a time to build up;
⁴ a time to weep, and a time to laugh;
    a time to mourn, and a time to dance;
⁵ a time to cast away stones,
    and a time to gather stones together;
        a time to embrace,
    and a time to refrain from embracing;

⁶a time to get, and a time to lose;
  a time to keep, and a time to cast away;
⁷a time to rend, and a time to sew;
  a time to keep silence, and a time to speak;
⁸a time to love, and a time to hate;
  a time of war, and a time of peace.
⁹What profit hath he
  that worketh in that wherein he laboureth?
¹⁰I have seen the travail,
  which God hath given to the sons of men
    to be exercised in it.
¹¹He hath made every thing beautiful in his time;
  also he hath set the world in their heart,
    so that no man can find out the work
  that God maketh from the beginning to the end.
¹²I know that there is no good in them,
  but for a man to rejoice,
    and to do good in his life.
¹³And also that every man should eat and drink,
  and enjoy the good of all his labour,
    it is the gift of God.
¹⁴I know that, whatsoever God doeth,
  it shall be for ever; nothing can be put to it,
    nor any thing taken from it;
  and God doeth it,
    that men should fear before him.
¹⁵That which hath been is now;
  and that which is to be hath already been;
    and God requireth that which is past.
¹⁶And moreover I saw under the sun

the place of judgment,
    that wickedness was there;
and the place of righteousness,
    that iniquity was there.
[17] I said in mine heart,
    "God shall judge the righteous and the wicked,
        for there is a time there
    for every purpose and for every work."
[18] I said in mine heart
    concerning the estate of the sons of men,
        that God might manifest them,
    and that they might see
        that they themselves are beasts.
[19] For that which befalleth the sons of men
    befalleth beasts;
        even one thing befalleth them.
    As the one dieth, so dieth the other;
        yea, they have all one breath;
    so that a man hath no preeminence above a beast,
        for all is vanity.
[20] All go unto one place; all are of the dust,
    and all turn to dust again.
[21] Who knoweth the spirit of man that goeth upward,
    and the spirit of the beast
        that goeth downward to the earth?
[22] Wherefore I perceive that there is nothing better,
    than that a man should rejoice in his own works,
        for that is his portion,
    for who shall bring him to see
        what shall be after him?

4
'So I returned, and considered all the oppressions
that are done under the sun;
and behold the tears of such as were oppressed,
and they had no comforter;
and on the side of their oppressors
there was power;
but they had no comforter.
² Wherefore I praised the dead which are already dead
more than the living which are yet alive.
³ Yea, better is he than both they,
which hath not yet been,
who hath not seen the evil work
that is done under the sun.
⁴ Again, I considered all travail, and every right work,
that for this a man is envied of his neighbour.
This is also vanity and vexation of spirit.
⁵ The fool foldeth his hands together,
and eateth his own flesh.
⁶ Better is an handful with quietness,
than both the hands full
with travail and vexation of spirit.
⁷ Then I returned, and I saw vanity under the sun.
⁸ There is one alone, and there is not a second;
yea, he hath neither child nor brother;
yet is there no end of all his labour;
neither is his eye satisfied with riches;
neither saith he, "For whom do I labour,
and bereave my soul of good?"
This is also vanity, yea, it is a sore travail.
⁹ Two are better than one,

because they have a good reward for their labour.
¹⁰ For if they fall, the one will lift up his fellow,
    but woe to him that is alone when he falleth;
        for he hath not another to help him up.
¹¹ Again, if two lie together, then they have heat,
    but how can one be warm alone?
¹² And if one prevail against him,
    two shall withstand him;
        and a threefold cord is not quickly broken.
¹³ Better is a poor and a wise child
    than an old and foolish king,
        who will no more be admonished.
¹⁴ For out of prison he cometh to reign;
    whereas also he that is born in his kingdom
        becometh poor.
¹⁵ I considered all the living which walk under the sun,
    with the second child
        that shall stand up in his stead.
¹⁶ There is no end of all the people,
    even of all that have been before them;
        they also that come after shall not rejoice in him.
    Surely this also is vanity and vexation of spirit.

5   'Keep thy foot when thou goest to the house of God,
        and be more ready to hear,
            than to give the sacrifice of fools,
        for they consider not that they do evil.
² Be not rash with thy mouth,
        and let not thine heart be hasty
            to utter any thing before God,

for God is in heaven, and thou upon earth;
therefore let thy words be few.
³ For a dream cometh
through the multitude of business;
and a fool's voice
is known by multitude of words.
⁴ When thou vowest a vow unto God,
defer not to pay it;
for he hath no pleasure in fools.
Pay that which thou hast vowed.
⁵ Better is it that thou shouldest not vow,
than that thou shouldest vow and not pay.
⁶ Suffer not thy mouth to cause thy flesh to sin;
neither say thou before the angel,
that it was an error.
Wherefore should God be angry at thy voice,
and destroy the work of thine hands?
⁷ For in the multitude of dreams and many words
there are also divers vanities, but fear thou God.
⁸ If thou seest the oppression of the poor,
and violent perverting of judgment
and justice in a province,
marvel not at the matter,
for he that is higher than the highest regardeth;
and there be higher than they.
⁹ Moreover the profit of the earth is for all;
the king himself is served by the field.
¹⁰ He that loveth silver shall not be satisfied with silver;
nor he that loveth abundance with increase;
this is also vanity.

¹¹ When goods increase,
>> they are increased that eat them,
>>> and what good is there to the owners thereof,
>> saving the beholding of them with their eyes?

¹² The sleep of a labouring man is sweet,
>> whether he eat little or much,
>>> but the abundance of the rich
>> will not suffer him to sleep.

¹³ There is a sore evil which I have seen
>> under the sun, namely,
>>> riches kept for the owners thereof to their hurt.

¹⁴ But those riches perish by evil travail,
>> and he begetteth a son,
>>> and there is nothing in his hand.

¹⁵ As he came forth of his mother's womb,
>> naked shall he return to go as he came,
>>> and shall take nothing of his labour,
>> which he may carry away in his hand.

¹⁶ And this also is a sore evil,
>> that in all points as he came, so shall he go,
>>> and what profit hath he
>> that hath laboured for the wind?

¹⁷ All his days also he eateth in darkness,
>> and he hath much sorrow and wrath
>>> with his sickness.

¹⁸ Behold that which I have seen;
>> it is good and comely for one to eat and to drink,
>>> and to enjoy the good of all his labour
>> that he taketh under the sun
>>> all the days of his life, which God giveth him,

for it is his portion.

¹⁹ Every man also to whom God hath given
    riches and wealth,
        and hath given him power to eat thereof,
    and to take his portion, and to rejoice in his labour;
        this is the gift of God.

²⁰ For he shall not much remember the days of his life;
    because God answereth him in the joy of his heart.

6 ¹ There is an evil which I have seen under the sun,
    and it is common among men:

² A man to whom God hath given riches,
    wealth, and honour,
        so that he wanteth nothing for his soul
    of all that he desireth,
        yet God giveth him not power to eat thereof,
    but a stranger eateth it;
        this is vanity, and it is an evil disease.

³ If a man beget an hundred children,
    and live many years,
        so that the days of his years be many,
    and his soul be not filled with good,
        and also that he have no burial,
    I say, that an untimely birth is better than he.

⁴ For he cometh in with vanity,
    and departeth in darkness,
        and his name shall be covered with darkness.

⁵ Moreover he hath not seen the sun,
    nor known any thing;
        this hath more rest than the other.

⁶ Yea, though he live a thousand years twice told,
yet hath he seen no good:
do not all go to one place?
⁷ All the labour of man is for his mouth,
and yet the appetite is not filled.
⁸ For what hath the wise more than the fool?
What hath the poor,
that knoweth to walk before the living?
⁹ Better is the sight of the eyes
than the wandering of the desire;
this is also vanity and vexation of spirit.
¹⁰ That which hath been is named already,
and it is known that it is man;
neither may he contend with him
that is mightier than he.
¹¹ Seeing there be many things that increase vanity,
what is man the better?
¹² For who knoweth what is good for man in this life,
all the days of his vain life
which he spendeth as a shadow?
For who can tell a man
what shall be after him under the sun?

7   ʼA good name is better than precious ointment;
and the day of death than the day of one's birth.
² It is better to go to the house of mourning,
than to go to the house of feasting,
for that is the end of all men;
and the living will lay it to his heart.
³ Sorrow is better than laughter,

for by the sadness of the countenance
   the heart is made better.
⁴ The heart of the wise is in the house of mourning;
   but the heart of fools is in the house of mirth.
⁵ It is better to hear the rebuke of the wise,
   than for a man to hear the song of fools.
⁶ For as the crackling of thorns under a pot,
   so is the laughter of the fool; this also is vanity.
⁷ Surely oppression maketh a wise man mad;
   and a gift destroyeth the heart.
⁸ Better is the end of a thing than the beginning thereof:
   and the patient in spirit
      is better than the proud in spirit.
⁹ Be not hasty in thy spirit to be angry,
   for anger resteth in the bosom of fools.
¹⁰ Say not thou, "What is the cause
   that the former days were better than these?"
      for thou dost not enquire wisely concerning this.
¹¹ Wisdom is good with an inheritance,
   and by it there is profit to them that see the sun.
¹² For wisdom is a defence, and money is a defence,
   but the excellency of knowledge is,
      that wisdom giveth life to them that have it.
¹³ Consider the work of God,
   for who can make that straight,
      which he hath made crooked?
¹⁴ In the day of prosperity be joyful,
   but in the day of adversity consider:
      God also hath set the one over against the other,
      to the end that man should find nothing after him.

¹⁵All things have I seen in the days of my vanity:
   there is a just man that perisheth
      in his righteousness,
   and there is a wicked man
      that prolongeth his life in his wickedness.
¹⁶Be not righteous over much;
   neither make thyself over wise;
      why shouldest thou destroy thyself?
¹⁷Be not over much wicked, neither be thou foolish;
   why shouldest thou die before thy time?
¹⁸It is good that thou shouldest take hold of this;
   yea, also from this withdraw not thine hand,
      for he that feareth God
   shall come forth of them all.
¹⁹Wisdom strengtheneth the wise
   more than ten mighty men which are in the city.
²⁰For there is not a just man upon earth,
   that doeth good, and sinneth not.
²¹Also take no heed unto all words that are spoken,
   lest thou hear thy servant curse thee:
²²For oftentimes also thine own heart knoweth
   that thou thyself likewise hast cursed others.
²³All this have I proved by wisdom;
   I said, "I will be wise," but it was far from me.
²⁴That which is far off, and exceeding deep,
   who can find it out?
²⁵I applied mine heart to know, and to search,
   and to seek out wisdom, and the reason of things,
      and to know the wickedness of folly,
   even of foolishness and madness.

[26]And I find more bitter than death the woman,
  whose heart is snares and nets,
    and her hands as bands;
  whoso pleaseth God shall escape from her;
    but the sinner shall be taken by her.'
[27]'Behold, this have I found,' saith the Preacher,
  'counting one by one, to find out the account,
[28]which yet my soul seeketh, but I find not.
  One man among a thousand have I found;
    but a woman among all those have I not found.
[29]Lo, this only have I found,
  that God hath made man upright;
    but they have sought out many inventions.

8 'Who is as the wise man?
    And who knoweth the interpretation of a thing?
      A man's wisdom maketh his face to shine,
    and the boldness of his face shall be changed.
[2]I counsel thee to keep the king's commandment,
    and that in regard of the oath of God.
[3]Be not hasty to go out of his sight:
    stand not in an evil thing;
      for he doeth whatsoever pleaseth him.
[4]Where the word of a king is, there is power,
    and who may say unto him, "What doest thou?"
[5]Whoso keepeth the commandment
    shall feel no evil thing and a wise man's heart
      discerneth both time and judgment.
[6]Because to every purpose there is time and judgment,
    therefore the misery of man is great upon him.

⁷ For he knoweth not that which shall be;
  for who can tell him when it shall be?
⁸ There is no man that hath power over the spirit
  to retain the spirit;
      neither hath he power in the day of death,
  and there is no discharge in that war;
      neither shall wickedness deliver those
  that are given to it.
⁹ All this have I seen, and applied my heart
  unto every work that is done under the sun.
      There is a time wherein
  one man ruleth over another to his own hurt.
¹⁰ And so I saw the wicked buried,
  who had come and gone from the place of the holy,
      and they were forgotten in the city
  where they had so done; this is also vanity.
¹¹ Because sentence against an evil work
  is not executed speedily,
      therefore the heart of the sons of men
  is fully set in them to do evil.
¹² Though a sinner do evil an hundred times,
  and his days be prolonged,
      yet surely I know that it shall be well
  with them that fear God, which fear before him.
¹³ But it shall not be well with the wicked,
  neither shall he prolong his days,
      which are as a shadow;
  because he feareth not before God.
¹⁴ There is a vanity which is done upon the earth;
  that there be just men unto whom it happeneth

according to the work of the wicked;
again, there be wicked men, to whom it happeneth
according to the work of the righteous;
I said that this also is vanity.
¹⁵ Then I commended mirth,
because a man hath no better thing under the sun,
than to eat, and to drink, and to be merry:
for that shall abide with him
of his labour the days of his life,
which God giveth him under the sun.
¹⁶ When I applied mine heart to know wisdom,
and to see the business that is done upon the earth
(for also there is that neither day
nor night seeth sleep with his eyes),
¹⁷ then I beheld all the work of God,
that a man cannot find out the work
that is done under the sun:
because though a man labour to seek it out,
yet he shall not find it;
yea further; though a wise man think to know it,
yet shall he not be able to find it.

9 'For all this I considered in my heart
even to declare all this, that the righteous,
and the wise, and their works,
are in the hand of God;
no man knoweth either love or hatred
by all that is before them.
²All things come alike to all;
there is one event to the righteous,

and to the wicked;
to the good and to the clean, and to the unclean;
to him that sacrificeth,
and to him that sacrificeth not:
as is the good, so is the sinner;
and he that sweareth, as he that feareth an oath.
³ This is an evil among all things
that are done under the sun,
that there is one event unto all;
yea, also the heart of the sons of men is full of evil,
and madness is in their heart while they live,
and after that they go to the dead.
⁴ For to him that is joined to all the living there is hope,
for a living dog is better than a dead lion.
⁵ For the living know that they shall die,
but the dead know not any thing,
neither have they any more a reward;
for the memory of them is forgotten.
⁶ Also their love, and their hatred, and their envy,
is now perished;
neither have they any more a portion
for ever in any thing that is done under the sun.
⁷ Go thy way, eat thy bread with joy,
and drink thy wine with a merry heart;
for God now accepteth thy works.
⁸ Let thy garments be always white;
and let thy head lack no ointment.
⁹ Live joyfully with the wife whom thou lovest
all the days of the life of thy vanity,
which he hath given thee under the sun,

all the days of thy vanity,
>for that is thy portion in this life,
and in thy labour which thou takest under the sun.
¹⁰ Whatsoever thy hand findeth to do,
>do it with thy might;
>>for there is no work, nor device,
nor knowledge, nor wisdom, in the grave,
>whither thou goest.
¹¹ I returned, and saw under the sun,
>that the race is not to the swift,
>>nor the battle to the strong,
neither yet bread to the wise,
>nor yet riches to men of understanding,
nor yet favour to men of skill;
>but time and chance happeneth to them all.
¹² For man also knoweth not his time,
>as the fishes that are taken in an evil net,
>>and as the birds that are caught in the snare;
so are the sons of men snared in an evil time,
>when it falleth suddenly upon them.
¹³ This wisdom have I seen also under the sun,
>and it seemed great unto me.
¹⁴ There was a little city, and few men within it;
>and there came a great king against it,
>>and besieged it,
and built great bulwarks against it.
¹⁵ Now there was found in it a poor wise man,
>and he by his wisdom delivered the city;
>>yet no man remembered that same poor man.
¹⁶ Then said I, "Wisdom is better than strength:

nevertheless the poor man's wisdom is despised,
  and his words are not heard."
[17] The words of wise men are heard in quiet more
  than the cry of him that ruleth among fools.
[18] Wisdom is better than weapons of war;
  but one sinner destroyeth much good.

10 [1]Dead flies cause the ointment of the apothecary
  to send forth a stinking savour;
    so doth a little folly him
  that is in reputation for wisdom and honour.
[2]A wise man's heart is at his right hand;
  but a fool's heart at his left.
[3] Yea also, when he that is a fool walketh by the way,
  his wisdom faileth him,
    and he saith to every one that he is a fool.
[4] If the spirit of the ruler rise up against thee,
  leave not thy place,
    for yielding pacifieth great offences.
[5] There is an evil which I have seen under the sun,
  as an error which proceedeth from the ruler:
[6] folly is set in great dignity,
  and the rich sit in low place.
[7] I have seen servants upon horses,
  and princes walking as servants upon the earth.
[8] He that diggeth a pit shall fall into it;
  and whoso breaketh an hedge,
    a serpent shall bite him.
[9] Whoso removeth stones shall be hurt therewith;
  and he that cleaveth wood

shall be endangered thereby.

¹⁰ If the iron be blunt, and he do not whet the edge,
    then must he put to more strength,
        but wisdom is profitable to direct.

¹¹ Surely the serpent will bite without enchantment;
    and a babbler is no better.

¹² The words of a wise man's mouth are gracious;
    but the lips of a fool will swallow up himself.

¹³ The beginning of the words of his mouth
    is foolishness,
        and the end of his talk is mischievous madness.

¹⁴ A fool also is full of words.
    A man cannot tell what shall be;
        and what shall be after him, who can tell him?

¹⁵ The labour of the foolish wearieth every one of them,
    because he knoweth not how to go to the city.

¹⁶ Woe to thee, O land, when thy king is a child,
    and thy princes eat in the morning!

¹⁷ Blessed art thou, O land,
    when thy king is the son of nobles,
        and thy princes eat in due season,
    for strength, and not for drunkenness!

¹⁸ By much slothfulness the building decayeth;
    and through idleness of the hands
        the house droppeth through.

¹⁹ A feast is made for laughter,
    and wine maketh merry,
        but money answereth all things.

²⁰ Curse not the king, no not in thy thought;
    and curse not the rich in thy bedchamber,

for a bird of the air shall carry the voice,
and that which hath wings shall tell the matter.

11 'Cast thy bread upon the waters,
for thou shalt find it after many days.
[2] Give a portion to seven, and also to eight;
for thou knowest not what evil
shall be upon the earth.
[3] If the clouds be full of rain,
they empty themselves upon the earth,
and if the tree fall toward the south,
or toward the north,
in the place where the tree falleth, there it shall be.
[4] He that observeth the wind shall not sow;
and he that regardeth the clouds shall not reap.
[5] As thou knowest not what is the way of the spirit,
nor how the bones do grow
in the womb of her that is with child,
even so thou knowest not
the works of God who maketh all.
[6] In the morning sow thy seed,
and in the evening withhold not thine hand,
for thou knowest not whether shall prosper,
either this or that,
or whether they both shall be alike good.
[7] Truly the light is sweet, and a pleasant thing it is
for the eyes to behold the sun.
[8] But if a man live many years, and rejoice in them all,
yet let him remember the days of darkness,
for they shall be many.

All that cometh is vanity.
⁹ Rejoice, O young man, in thy youth;
        and let thy heart cheer thee in the days of thy youth,
                and walk in the ways of thine heart,
                and in the sight of thine eyes:
                        but know thou, that for all these things
                God will bring thee into judgment.
¹⁰ Therefore remove sorrow from thy heart,
        and put away evil from thy flesh,
                for childhood and youth are vanity.

12 ¹Remember now thy Creator in the days of thy youth,
        while the evil days come not,
                nor the years draw nigh, when thou shalt say,
        "I have no pleasure in them,"
² while the sun, or the light, or the moon,
        or the stars, be not darkened,
                nor the clouds return after the rain;
³ in the day when the keepers of the house shall tremble,
        and the strong men shall bow themselves,
                and the grinders cease because they are few,
        and those that look out of the windows
                be darkened,
⁴ and the doors shall be shut in the streets,
        when the sound of the grinding is low,
                and he shall rise up at the voice of the bird,
                and all the daughters of musick shall be brought low;
⁵ also when they shall be afraid of that which is high,
        and fears shall be in the way,
                and the almond tree shall flourish,

and the grasshopper shall be a burden,
    and desire shall fail,
because man goeth to his long home,
    and the mourners go about the streets;
⁶ or ever the silver cord be loosed,
    or the golden bowl be broken,
        or the pitcher be broken at the fountain,
        or the wheel broken at the cistern.
⁷ Then shall the dust return to the earth as it was,
    and the spirit shall return unto God who gave it.
⁸ Vanity of vanities,' saith the preacher. 'All is vanity.'
⁹ And moreover, because the preacher was wise,
    he still taught the people knowledge;
        yea, he gave good heed, and sought out,
    and set in order many proverbs.
¹⁰ The preacher sought to find out acceptable words,
    and that which was written was upright,
        even words of truth.
¹¹ The words of the wise are as goads,
    and as nails fastened by the masters of assemblies,
        which are given from one shepherd.
¹² And further, by these, my son, be admonished;
    of making many books there is no end;
        and much study is a weariness of the flesh.
¹³ Let us hear the conclusion of the whole matter:
    Fear God, and keep his commandments,
        for this is the whole duty of man.
¹⁴ For God shall bring every work into judgment,
    with every secret thing,
        whether it be good, or whether it be evil.

titles in the series